PURSUING THE
DREAM

JEAN BOVELL

Published by Jean Bovell 2020

Copyright © Jean Bovell 2020

All rights reserved. No part of this publication may be reproduced, stored in a retrieval system, or transmitted in any form or by any means, electronic, mechanical, photocopy, recording or otherwise, without prior written permission of the copyright owner. Nor can it be circulated in any form of binding or cover other than that in which it is published and without similar condition including this condition being imposed on a subsequent purchaser

ISBN 978-1-911412-99-1

Published by Dolman Scott
www.dolmanscott.co.uk

PROLOGUE

Pursuing The Dream

Stephen Lewis was born in London to parents who are members of the Windrush Generation. Throughout his life, Stephen has been an avid reader, with a passion for acquiring knowledge on different topics of interest. But he is especially intrigued by his Caribbean heritage, and in that pursuit, pored over various related publications and viewed documentaries that featured the experiences of West Indians of the period, before and after they arrived in the United Kingdom. Stephen was, however, unable to uncover anything that may have been documented about the actual 19-day journey experience across the Atlantic Ocean.

Inspired by the long held curiosities of Stephen Lewis, the narrative shines light on a "once-upon-a-time" era, prior to achieving independence from Britain, when English-speaking people from the Caribbean considered themselves British and were proud to be subjects of the realm. It speaks of individuals who dreamt of a better life for themselves and their family, and as a consequence, did not hesitate in stepping forward when people from the various colonised West Indian islands were being recruited by Britain to assist with rebuilding the country after the ravishes of World War Two. Although they embraced what was envisaged as the once-in-a-lifetime opportunity to earn "big money" for services rendered, the vast majority planned to return "home" following a duration of five years.

Based on fact, this particular trip being taken to the United Kingdom by Caribbean Pioneers is centred on a liner that is representative of the method of affordable transportation across the Atlantic back then.

The names, physical characteristics and personalities featured are fictional. The separate disclosures, and the events, situations and scenarios described, are being sensationalised and designed to impact the imagination of the reader. However, the narrative largely echoes the true testimony of some of the people who travelled to London, albeit on separate Italian steamships, during the late 1950s and early 1960s. The consensus lasting memory being expressed in just one conclusive sentence: "We had a real good time on the boat."

PURSUING THE DREAM is a compilation of separate but inter-related human stories that reflects the different encounters between individuals during an enclosed three-week journey across the Atlantic. Written on a backdrop of the overall experience, and inclusive of historical themes and geographical factors, the author endeavours to capture the essence of the time when a life-changing leap of faith was being taken by a generation of young West Indian men and women with the collective dream of a better life.

Jean Bovell

Acknowledgements

J. Baptiste

M. Francis

P. Jeremiah

L. Lansequot

P. Lett

D. Lewis

S. Lewis

M.A. Mason

G. Mason

J. Plange

I. Radix

Special thanks to
J. Mackintosh for his technical contribution.

Geographical and historical content accessed via
on-line research

Content

Boats In Caribbean Waters Back Then 1
See You In Five Years 3
Life Changing Journey Begins 9
Long And Eventful First Day 14
Stowaways On Board 26
Getting Into The Swing 28
Discord And Altercation 30
An Unlikely Pairing 32
Family Connection Uncovered 40
Fascinating Woman 48
No Ordinary Day 54
Return Of The Good Times 57
The Outsiders 60
Having Fun At The Competitions 64
Tragedy Strikes 73
The Other Side Of The Ocean 79
The Final Hurrah 84
Unforgettable Journey Ends 86
London Is The Place For Me 87

Boats In Caribbean Waters Back Then

The traffic of passenger liners, steamships, oil tankers and various large boats that transported people, manufactured goods and general commodities to and from the Americas and the Caribbean and across the Atlantic had always been commonplace in Caribbean waters. But the economy of the region had also been dependent on the reliable services provided by local franchise or independently owned large and small boats. The vessels were necessary not only for maintaining the flow of lucrative trading of merchandise and natural produce between the islands, but also enabled abundant profitable fishing within the surrounding fertile waters. Moreover, "windjammers", as they were often called, had been the vessels largely hired for the purposes of short pleasure cruises, island-hopping trips and ferrying individuals on visits to relatives and friends who lived on different islands.

Apart from the various exported products such as Box ide, cocoa and spices, as is currently the case, the Caribbean of an era had been particularly known for producing and exporting bananas across the globe. Back then, this was echoed in the catchy sing-along popular West Indian folk song that was regularly played on local radio and sung by many individuals throughout the region. The lyrics – "DAY 0! DayaaO! Daylight come and me wanna go Ooome. Day de de day, de de day, dayaaO, daylight come and me wanna go home!" – referred to exhausted labourers who were anxious to return to their homes at the crack of dawn following a night spent loading bananas onto boats. These refrigerated vessels, commonly known as "Banana Boats", were used by Banana Traders to speedily carry the nutritious but fast-ripening fruit from the islands to North America and countries across the Atlantic.

Banana Boats also provided a special service to the England Cricket Team by economically transporting them to the particular islands on which matches were scheduled, such as Jamaica, Barbados, Trinidad and Guyana, during their tour of the West Indies in the 1950s. It could not have been at that time imagined that the named vessels would one day become the basis for the contentious opinions being directed towards West Indians who entered the UK during the period. "They fell off the Banana Boat!" was alleged to have been a common derogatory comment expressed by various members of the then host community.

See You In Five Years

The post-war era gave rise to what would result in an historical turning-point in the lives of many young adults who resided in the colonised English-speaking Caribbean islands such as Jamaica, Barbados, Dominica, Grenada, St Lucia and Trinidad and Tobago. West Indians of the day believed they were British, and were staunchly loyal and patriotic to the "Mother Country". Therefore, many young men from the Caribbean felt an obligation to answer the call of duty by serving in the British Air Force or British Navy, alongside other allied forces during World Wars One and Two.

When Britain asked for assistance with rebuilding the country following the ravishes of World War Two, the request would result in a huge response from under-privileged young West Indians who had harboured the dream of a better life. It had been for them all the chance of a life-time that they were being enabled to be hugely rewarded for carrying out the tasks required. Some may even have imagined being offered career opportunities. Permanent residence in the United Kingdom was not, however, envisaged by "fortune seekers". They planned to live and work in the "land of promise" for a maximum of five years, by which time they should have accumulated sufficient funds for "going back home", building a "big house" and generally ensuring a more comfortable lifestyle for themselves and their family. Consequently, "see you in five years!!!!" may have been the parting words to extended and close family members by many who decided to take this significant leap of faith.

Neither the idea of being transported to England on a "Banana Boat" nor, at the opposite end of the spectrum, being passengers on a "five-star" luxurious Cunard Ocean Liner would have entered the psyche of those who had decided to embark on the long journey by sea to the United Kingdom. Indeed, the young adventurers would most likely have travelled on one of the various Italian steamships of the period that provided an affordable cabin-class service between the Caribbean and the Italian port of Genoa, inclusive of connecting services to a specified train station in London.

Migrants from the island of Grenada scheduled to travel to London on one such vessel in October 1961, would have undoubtedly been impacted by the tragedy that occurred on their shores only a few months previously.

Sunday, July 22nd 1961 had been expected to be just another uneventful sleepy day of rest when the majority attended Church Services, ate well and engaged in various forms of leisure activity. But no one, and in particular the people who resided within the small city of St George, would have imagined that a relatively minor incident that occurred on a ship docked in nearby waters would unexpectedly erupt into a catastrophic event that would completely shatter their easy-going and tranquil environment.

It was approximately 9.30 on that particular Sunday morning, a time when, apart from essential workers, locals may have been returning from Church, enjoying a lavish breakfast, being involved in some form of activity or simply going about their business, when they were suddenly and unexpectedly startled by an alarming series of thunderous sounds that boomed across the town. The explosions were accompanied by raging red flames and thick black smoke that could be seen rising high above the passenger liner *Bianca C* that had been docked in the city's outer harbour. The immediately raised alarm was quickly followed by hastily expedited Emergency Services. Owners of large and small vessels moored in nearby waters or local marinas also sprang into action by speeding towards the burning structure in a desperate mission to rescue as many people as possible.

The combined rescue operation carried out on the fateful day had been largely successful. Of the three hundred and sixty-four passengers on board the *Bianca C* at the time of the accident, one person was confirmed to have been killed outright by the blast and one other was declared missing. However, three hundred and sixty-two individuals, including fifteen who had boarded the ship from Grenada, were rescued from the raging inferno. The lives of three hundred and eleven crew members were also saved, and medical care and welfare assistance was provided by the authorities. But many people who lived in the local area also rallied to help and provided food, comfort and shelter to a large number of un-injured but traumatised passengers.

Despite having succeeded in saving the lives of the majority who were on board the *Bianca C* when the fire flared, the Grenada authorities struggled with controlling the huge blaze. Their efforts appeared to have had little effect on significantly minimising the furious flames and thick smoke that continuously raged from the ship.

Local fire-fighters had not previously been faced with the task of quenching such an overwhelming blaze, but moreover, did not possess the required equipment or appropriately trained operators. Assistance was, as a consequence, requested from the British frigate, HMS *Londonderry*, at that time stationed on the island of Puerto Rico. The response was quickly expedited and subsequent to arriving on the scene, a comprehensive assessment of the situation was carried out. It resulted in the decision that the burning vessel would be towed to a safe location prior to executing the complex task of extinguishing the flames. Unfortunately, after six hours and just three miles into the process, the tow-line snapped and within seconds the *Bianca C* sank and vanished beneath the sea.

An enquiry into the tragedy was subsequently convened. It was established that the explosions and huge fires that erupted on the *Bianca C* on July 22nd 1961 had been ignited by a small flame that originated in the ship's engine room.

The following months flew by and it seemed that in very little time the day of departure to London had arrived for those who were booked to travel to London on a particular date in October 1961. And it was with feelings of intense excitement tinged with sadness about the prospect of having to say good-bye to close relatives and friends, that individuals waited in anticipation to board the Steam Ship that would take them to the envisaged land of plenty. But beneath the charged atmosphere of mixed emotions, lay concerns of potential risks that were associated with the recent catastrophic events that unfolded on the vessel, Bianca C.

The expectations held by these Caribbean pioneers had been based on the colonial dictate that instilled within their being a sense of patriotism and belonging to the Great British Empire headed by the Queen of England. Many of the generation would have recalled an education based on the English Curriculum and being schooled on a diet of British history. In particular, the celebration of "Empire Day" had been a national annual ritual. Clad in crisply laundered uniform, children from different schools would march in the presence of the Governor, the Queen's representative on the island, and in tune with a Marching Police Band, passionately deliver the patriotic anthem: "Rule Britannia. Britannia rule the waves!"

It would have been due to these factors that individuals who craved better opportunities in the United Kingdom did not consider themselves immigrants. On the contrary, their sense of belonging to the British Empire may have been bolstered by being in possession of an "entitled" British passport as they waited to embark on the journey to London, accompanied by close relatives and friends who were at the pier to "see them off". But it would be after much heartfelt and tearful farewell embraces with loved ones that those who were about to set off on a new adventure stepped into the small boats that would take them to the Italian steamship that was docked in the city's outer harbour. Despite being distressed by thoughts of having to leave loved ones behind, they were nonetheless heartened by loud expressed sentiments of best wishes ringing in their ears as they sailed towards the large vessel that would take them to their destination. "Safe journey!", "We'll be praying for you!", "Good luck!", "See you in five years!"

On entering the main ship, the new passengers were required to present their passports and travel documents for investigation and important information was registered, prior to being directed to designated cabins most of which were situated below the lower deck. This particular vessel had just two decks. The cabins which were adequately furnished, contained two separate pairs of bunk beds and en-suite, bathroom facilities, appeared to have been designed to accommodate four individuals of the same sex. After relieving themselves of their luggage, those who recently joined the ship hurried back onto the upper deck and wormed their way through the throng of previously boarded passengers, with the desire to identify and wave final goodbyes to close family members and friends at the sea-front.

Within a short period of time, deafening sounds from the ship's horn and plumes of thick black smoke bellowing from the engines, signalled that the vessel was ready to depart on the journey across the Atlantic. And it was on a background of loudly expressed final good-byes and frantic waving between passengers and loved ones left behind, that the "floating hotel" manoeuvred from the island's outer harbour and sailed towards open waters. But it was not until the island became a tiny dot in the distance and eventually vanished, that the recently embarked passengers had been overwhelmed by deep feelings of melancholy that were associated with being parted from everyone and everything they had known and loved. And it was with heavy hearts that many individuals returned to their allocated economy cabins, in which they would be based for the next three weeks.

Life Changing Journey Begins

Steam Ship of the period

The highly anticipated trip of a life-time had at long last begun; but having never previously experienced a long journey on a relatively large ship, the newly boarded passengers harboured no particular expectation. However, they were resigned to the fact that the vessel on which they now stood would be "home", for better or worse, until it arrived at the final destination on the other side of the Atlantic. The reality of it all may have been a little daunting for the majority, who had taken only short trips on windjammers, to and from specific islands that lay in Caribbean waters. However, in spite of the enduring apprehension associated with the actual journey experience, it was for them all a worthwhile leap of faith.

Although the passengers came from the British Colonised West Indian islands and identified as British, each island had its own sub-culture, custom, method of speech and way of life. Consequently, those who recently boarded the vessel were quickly aware that they had entered a diverse environment that contained people from a variety of islands which may have included Dominica, Jamaica, St Lucia and Trinidad and Tobago.

The recently boarded passengers from the island of Grenada may have included several groups of friends or relatives, who had decided on travelling together. But of the various individuals that were unaccompanied, were four young women who were placed in a single cabin. Although they had not previously known each other, the new occupants were happy that they originated from the same country and shared a familiar culture. They may even have spotted each other while waiting at the island's harbour, but acknowledged that everyone was at the time focusing on spending precious moments with close family members and friends. Following mutual introductions, the women – now known to be Agatha, Sheila, Melrose and Olive – wasted no time in revealing to each other how exhausted they felt and for which various reasons were given. It may have been due to an all-night farewell party, restless sleeping, or an early start and/or a long "drive to catch the boat". However, everyone disclosed feelings of extreme hunger and wondered how long they would have to wait for dinner.

In the meantime, the women would in turn refresh themselves in the adjoining bathroom, before climbing into separately chosen bunk-beds. But were quietly resting when they were suddenly and unexpectedly stirred by the eagerly awaited announcement that supper was being served to "West Indian" passengers. These particular cabin-mates would be among many other newly boarded passengers with rumbling stomachs who hurried to the specified dining lounge. On arrival, it was immediately observed that diners seated on separate tables were already tucking into their meal, and Agatha, Sheila, Melrose and Olive would waste little time in grabbing themselves a vacant table, around which they all sat. Within minutes of being seated, large plates containing ample portions of meat, rice and vegetables, accompanied by glasses of red wine and non-alcoholic beverages, and followed by a variety of fresh fruit, were being provided by friendly servers. And after polishing off every morsel of food that had been placed on their table, the satisfied women were unanimous in their expressed critique of their very first meal on board ship. "I enjoyed it", "Very tasty", "It was really good", "And so much!" But the conversation would evolve eventually into the spontaneous sharing of background experiences and personal aspirations and dreams.

Agatha, a resident of St Andrew who appeared as a calm and pleasant 36-year-old woman, revealed that she was going to London to join her husband of ten years. Agatha went on to say that even though she was looking forward to reuniting with him, her heart ached for the couple's three children that had been placed in the care of their maternal grandmother. She did not doubt that the children would be well looked after: Grannie was all the same a stern, no-nonsense character who was quick to deliver physical punishment. However, the children had been reassured that their parents would return home within five years, having both worked and accumulated the funds necessary for building a "big house" where they would all live happily together. In the meantime, they would be sent regular parcels filled with nice outfits, toys and sweets.

Melrose, aged 43, who hailed from the parish of St Patrick, appeared tense and agitated, but in resigned tones remarked on how "lucky" Agatha was, before divulging the fact that she had been fleeing an abusive husband. Melrose went on to explain that she endured fifteen years of maltreatment from a selfish and domineering husband who was "hell" to live with, and that she had reached breaking point when her older sister, Hilda, who ran a small business, came up with a solution by offering to fund Melrose's trip to England. Hilda also vowed to keep an eye on the siblings who had been left in the care of their father. But Melrose added that she hoped to be reunited with the couple's offspring at some point after establishing a new life in London.

The youngest among the group was called Sheila. She presented as a demure and petite 19-year old, with a friendly disposition. Sheila, whose family resided in the parish of St John, said that having left school with high grades, she was being sent to London by her parents to "study nursing". Sheila went on to say that she would be staying with a relative and hoped to eventually qualify as a midwife.

Twenty-six-year-old Olive was a beautiful, vivacious young lady from a suburb in the City of St George, and with her dazzling smile and bubbly personality, appeared to be the happiest female in the group. In confident tones, Olive disclosed that she was on her way to marry the love of her life. "Ar can't wait!" she screamed excitedly, before proudly producing a snapshot of a handsome young man, which was passed around and scrutinised by the other three ladies, none of whom concealed their admiration for the dashing suitor. "What a handsome boy!", "Where yuh pick-up dis nice man?", "He is so good-looking!"

"He was me boyfriend, since in school," gushed Olive in response. But he "went up to" England last year, she added.

"Ar bet it will be pure electricity when all-yuh meet up," teased Agatha. Tickled by the double-meaning comment and feeling cheerfully inebriated after consuming large quantities of wine, the women simultaneously burst into uncontrollable laughter and held on to each other as they swayed sharply from one side to the other, while attempting to remain firmly seated. But there could be no denying that the process of a friendship bond was being created between the women following their separate personal disclosures. And even though they would have had no say in relation to the size or location their cabin, or with whom it should be occupied, these particular cabin-mates could not have been happier with the choices that had been made on their behalf.

The open but jolly interactions continued, and ended only when Olive complained of feeling dizzy. The "sisters" realised that they may have been somewhat over-indulgent with the wine as they staggered unsteadily but merrily towards their cabin. On entering, they immediately collapsed onto separate bunk-beds and very soon slipped into deep slumber. They were, as a consequence, oblivious to the different noisy but jolly sounds that persisted late into the night within various areas of the ship.

Long And Eventful First Day

Ocean View

The women would be abruptly woken from their sleep the following morning by deafening ringing sounds, accompanied by a directive that penetrated throughout their cabin: Everyone on deck! Everyone on deck! Everyone on deck! Fearing that they were in some form of danger, the cabin-mates scrambled out of bed and frantically pulled on their dresses, all the while uttering words of prayer. "Oh my God! Oh my God! Help us, please! Please help!" But they were about to make their exit, when it became apparent that Olive had not risen from the upper bunk in which she slept. "Olive! Olive! Get up! Get up! Come on!" they urged. Paralysed with terror, Olive was rooted to her bed and felt that she was unable to move her limbs. The alarming signals had ignited memories of the horrific explosions that occurred on the steamship *Bianca C* and reverberated through her home town of St George many months previously, and she assumed that the vessel on which she was now a passenger had been similarly afflicted. Olive was, as a consequence, stricken with profound feelings of dread.

Olive resided with her family within view of the city's outer harbour. She had heard the distressing noises and witnessed the rescue missions, and was convinced that history was being repeated and that she had unknowingly entered a doomed vessel. But the concerned cabin-mates would have been unaware of the basis for Olive's extreme anxieties as they unceremoniously pulled her out of bed, dressed and dragged her onto the upper deck as directed. On arrival, the ladies were relieved to discover that they, along with the other passengers, had been required to participate in nothing more serious than a routine safety drill. The worthwhile exercise included a step-by-step guide on how life-jackets should be fitted, rules for stepping into life-boats and methods that should be applied for gaining attention. Despite being thankful that her worst fears had not been realised, Olive would nonetheless remain emotionally unsettled for several hours subsequently.

On the way back to their cabin following the exercise, in which everyone on board had been involved, the women were approached by several young men. "Good morning. Yuh girls from Grenada?" asked a pleasant-looking member of the group.

"Yes," the women replied with smiling faces.

"We, too," said the young man. "They call me Anthony"; and, pointing in turn to his three companions, added: "And this is Gilbert, Lionel and Alfonso." Each person nodded in acknowledgement as their name was being mentioned. "We sharing a cabin," revealed Anthony. "All yuh ladies sharing one, too?"

"That's right!" trumped Agatha. On realising that they occupied adjoining cabins, everyone appeared pleasantly surprised, and they parted with friendly reciprocal words: "See you at breakfast!"

Although Olive continued to be somewhat affected by what was, for her, an unnerving early awakening, the young women had been in overall positive mood on returning to their cabin. They discussed the safety precaution drill and agreed that it had been beneficial to them all . "Yuh never know what could happen," said Madeline in solemn tones. "And if nothing else, they show us how to put on we life-jacket."

"That's true," replied the others collectively.

"So, how yuh feeling now, Olive?" asked Melrose.

"A lot better. Me heart ain't beating so fast. Arr tell yuh, it was a real relief that it wasn't anything serious."

"Leh we go an' bathe. Remember, we suppose to meet up with the boys for breakfast."

"That's right," came the unanimous response.

The experience of being involved in a life-saving exercise may have strengthened their developing bond, but the women appeared to be even more at ease in their shared environment, when they decided to show-case their treasured personally put-together new outfits. Indeed, very few retail outlets on their particular island of the period would have stocked ready-made garments, even so, these professionally made items may also have been largely unaffordable. However, the perfectly hand-made pieces included fitted mid-length dresses that emphasised the small-waisted, ample-bosomed figure considered appealing in those days, and colourful wide skirts with matching blouses and jackets. The ladies had been mindful also to include among their ensemble necessities for "keeping out the cold", such as stockings, appropriate footwear, raincoats, scarves, hats and gloves.

Before too long, the cabin-mates had responded to the call that breakfast was being served to West Indian passengers, and were seated around the table and tucking into separate choices, which may have been cereals, porridge, ham, eggs and buttered bread. But they would be suddenly distracted by the beaming faces of four young men hovering above them. "Can we join you, ladies?" Asked one of their number. "Of course! Bring all yuh chairs," came the collectively chimed reply. In no time at all, chairs were being noisily shifted around the medium-sized table as those already seated moved closer to each other in their endeavour to create space for accommodating the newcomers. Despite the squeeze, there was all-round delight that a slot had been found for everyone present. And it was with reciprocal broad smiles that the small talk began and continued over the meal, albeit limited to positive comments relating to the quality and quantity of the food. But gears were changed after everyone had finished eating, and the women began to converse about what they hoped to achieve in the "Mother Country". And it may have been because of the ladies' willingness to open up about their separate aspirations that the men decided that they also should disclose something of themselves.

Anthony, who was good-looking, well-groomed and relatively well-spoken, revealed that he was 28 years old and that he resided in the parish of St David, where he was born. As a result of being awarded an educational scholarship at the age of twelve, Anthony said that he was transferred from his local elementary school to an esteemed Boys Secondary School in the town of St George where he excelled in Mathematics, and after graduating took up a career in teaching. Anthony added that he had left a steady girlfriend behind and was missing her so much "already," but planned to "send for her" after finding a job and securing a base in London. Anthony further disclosed his long-term dream of entering university. "Hopefully Cambridge!" he exclaimed, optimistically.

"Cambridge? You wish!" retorted one member of the group in sceptical tones, echoing the thoughts of those with raised eyebrows who felt that Anthony had been aiming for the unreachable, but had chosen to remain silent. Nonetheless, he was eventually given an all-round "thumbs up" and wished success in his future endeavours.

Gilbert, on the other hand, had come up the hard way. He was a lean, casually dressed but self-effacing individual who had been raised in abject poverty in the parish of St Patrick. Gilbert disclosed that he left his local elementary school at just 14 years of age, as he was required to contribute towards the livelihood of his large family by working alongside his father and older brother in the fields. Although he was now married with a family of his own, Gilbert, now aged 36, continued to struggle. The chance of "going to England" and being able to earn a high wage had been an opportunity that could not be missed. It had been for him "God sent", and that relatives and friends contributed various amounts of money towards the purchase of his ticket to travel.

Although he expressed the hope of obtaining a well-paid job that would enable him to financially support his family back home, Gilbert revealed that his ultimate dream would be to return to his loved ones in five years' time, having accumulated sufficient cash for building a "big house" and generally providing a more comfortable lifestyle for them all. Everyone at the table nodded knowingly, indicating that they fully understood Gilbert's difficult life experiences and desire for a better life.

Lionel was a tall and heavily set individual. He wore thick glasses and his soft speaking tones were delivered in short, flurried bursts, emphasised by an expressively protruding chest and punctuated by fits of giggles so contagious that his audience could not help chuckling along with him. However, the manner in which Lionel turned his hand and loosely flipped his wrists during conversation may have been additional factors that brought smiles to everyone's faces.

Aged 40, Lionel explained that he had never been married, had no children of his own and always lived at home with his comparatively well-to-do parents. He was the only child of a couple who resided in a suburb of St George, known as Marianne. Both parents were career-minded and the family employed a maid. Lionel's father occupied a senior post in the Civil Service that required a fair amount of travel to other islands within the Eastern Caribbean Bloc, such as St Lucia, St Vincent and Dominica.

After leaving school, Lionel followed his father into the Civil Service. However, on arriving at his milestone 40th birthday, his father insisted that it was time he left home and begin to live independently. It was subsequently decided by both parents that England, with all its opportunities, would be the ideal place for their son to make a fresh start. They then purchased a ticket, packed his case, drove him to the harbour, embraced him, wished him Good Luck and waved him goodbye. Lionel went on to say that he had been saddened by the fact that he had more or less been "kicked out" of the family home, having not been allowed a "say" in the matter. There was, however, nothing he could do about it, and was now resigned to making the best of whatever the future had in store. "Maybe I'll get a job in the Civil Service over there," he remarked with a sigh of resignation. However, in spite of the sympathetic responses, and being transfixed by Lionel's engaging and charismatic persona, it was generally felt that at age 40, Lionel should have already left home and that his parents may have acted in his best interests.

Alfonso was a tall and athletic-looking twenty-something. Donned in the latest short-sleeved "jersey" that exposed well-toned muscular arms, Alfonso may have been considered a desirable catch by impressionable young females of his generation. But on flashing a broad smile that exhibited a prominently placed large gold tooth, it was plain to see that Alfonso was undeniably the stereotypical "Sweet Boy" of the day. Indeed, the seated ladies appeared spell-bound as they listened intently to his outpourings. Alfonso admitted to being somewhat of a "playboy", having already fathered five children with three different young ladies at just 23 years of age. He went on to profess, "tongue in cheek", that he should not be blamed for his remarkable conquests, claiming somewhat triumphantly that "dem women jes won't leave me alone!" The "cocky" assertion was, however, immediately followed by the admission that he was "only joking" and conceded that his dealings with women had been fundamentally irresponsible and reckless.

After completing his education at a Government-run elementary school, Alfonso, who had from a young age displayed a curiosity in all things mechanical, was immediately taken on as an apprentice mechanic by his uncle, who owned a vehicle repair business. He quickly learnt the required skills and very much enjoyed the work, even though it was often pressured. He was, however, "well rewarded" with "good money" for his efforts and was able to contribute "a little something" towards the upkeep of each of his offspring every month.

Alfonso revealed that he hoped to "get work in a garage", before enrolling at evening classes, where he intended to receive formal training in Mechanical Engineering. Alfonso planned to return home, start up a business and continue to support his children, but hoped that he would eventually settle down to family life with "a nice woman". It became apparent to those around the table that beneath the swagger was a thinking individual with a constructive plan for the future.

In spite of their unique stories and separate plans for the future, everyone around the particular table knew for certain that what they all had in common was the dream of a better life but they were also being reassured in the knowledge that they shared a familiar culture. These factors undoubtedly gave rise to a collective sense of belonging within the closed and diverse environment of the ship, and was the basis on which they decided to accompany each other on a tour around the ship. It would herald the beginning of a comradeship that continued throughout the rest of journey.

As the curious novices navigated their way along the different pathways on the two-deck ship, there seemed to be no escaping the persistent drone of engines and mechanical paraphernalia that penetrated the various areas, the never-ending traffic of passengers that were communicating with each other in raised voices, those who loitered, and the fresh breezes that wafted continuously across the upper and lower deck of the vessel. However, the group would discover that among the various facilities was a place for religious worship and a medical resource but they were particularly surprised when they came across a fairly large swimming pool that was positioned on the upper deck of the vessel.

No-one among the recently formed clique of friends had previously encountered and indoor pool. They may have assumed that only sea water or possibly rivers or lakes, had been designated places for swimming or even therapeutic purposes. In their culture, sea water or sulphur lakes were well-known for their healing properties. Moreover, underwater diving way out at sea had been a largely self-taught skill, executed without the aid of sophisticated breathing equipment and carried out primarily for the purpose of catching various species of shellfish such as lobster, Lambie, sea-eggs or even turtle. And a skilled occupation that provided a thriving business for those who reliably sold their "catch of the day" not only to enterprises such as hotels and restaurants, but also to members of the general public.

After lingering for a while at the pool-side, the stroll around the vessel would take the newcomers towards a section of the lower deck in which men were observed playing against each other at cricket or simply kicking a ball around, and women who were engaging in various exercise routines. On entering one of the lounges, several individuals of both sexes were spotted talking and laughing while standing around a bar with a drink in one hand and a "smoke" in the other. Others were seated on chairs around tables that overlooked the ocean and being occupied in some form of card or board game. Lone individuals appeared to be deep in thought as they sauntered around the upper or lower deck or quietly leant over the sides and gazed across the water while puffing and inhaling slowly on a cherished "ciggy."

Further into their tour around the ship, the group entered a large lounge in which there was a stage with a jukebox on either side. It was generally felt to be the main venue used for entertaining the passengers and an indication that good times should be expected. "So dis is where the music ar was hearing las nite was coming from?" Quipped Alfonso in distinctive patois tones. "Da good, cause ar love dancing."

"Me, too!" declared 36-year-old Agatha. The spontaneous enthusiastic response triggered immediate suspicion among her cabin-mates, "Looks like she fancy the man!" being the consensus whispered insinuation. Only time would no doubt tell if this slimmest of female hunches had been an astute glimpse into something that was yet to unfold.

As the companions continued to venture through the thoroughfare of travellers with radiant faces, they became aware that individuals "hung" with others from the same island and that people from French-speaking Caribbean islands such as Martinique and Guadeloupe were also in the mix. They were, however, unable to ignore crew members outfitted in casual but smart uniform, who were at all times vigilant and helpful. The pals' attention had also been drawn to stewards who seemed to be focused on surveying the ocean, and paused as they too rested their eyes upon the vast aquamarine waters and at that time, cloudless blue skies. And were awe-struck by the all-consuming infinity, sublimity and powerful sense of mystery engendered. But their concentration on the mystical surrounding was broken when they were distracted by a passing vessel. It seemed unbelievable to them all that the ship that had so swiftly overtaken them may well have been the blurred vison that had previously been observed hovering on the horizon. The overall wonderstruck moments were among many significant experiences that would be forever ingrained in the memory of these first-time travellers during their journey across the Atlantic.

Everyone was in high spirits as the companions headed for the bar after completing their walk around the ship, and before too long they were reflecting on the various accessible activities over a few drinks. But it was also acknowledged that the overall environment appeared care-free and suggestive of individuals being free to choose to do nothing at all, spend quality time with friends or simply mingle and get to know passengers from different islands. Indeed, this particular group of men and women had arrived at a juncture where any previously held uncertainties regarding the actual journey experience may have been cast aside as they looked forward to good times that appeared to be there for the taking.

The conversations were carried over onto the dining table as the friends later lunched together on a meal that had been given the "thumbs up" having judged to be "very tasty" and plentiful. But before parting ways, they would arrange to meet again at supper.

The recently formed circle of friends was in jovial mood and flashed toothy grins as they greeted each other with affectionate taps on the arm, on coming together at their exclusive table. Feeling relaxed and void of inhibitions, they chatted freely, shared hilarious jokes, laughed loudly and hysterically, and without knowing it, had integrated into the general atmospheric buzz of human interactions that included groups of individuals enjoying a "sing-song" around the dining table.

The jollies continued for the pals until the male members of the group suggested that they should carry on the fun by moving to the large lounge for an evening of entertainment. The women were, however, not keen on the idea. They were mindful of the fact that their journey had only just started and felt that there should be plenty of time ahead for taking in a show or dancing the night away. And decided to retire to their cabin following a long and eventful but tiring day.

Stowaways On Board

The next morning, as West Indian passengers were tucking into breakfast, a commotion, accompanied by alarming loud voices that seemed to be coming from deep beneath the lower deck, echoed across the dining lounge. And before too long, three dishevelled-looking young men, under the supervision of an equal number of stewards, came into view, and were being escorted to a vacant table. Needless to say, the incident drew the attention of those already seated, all of whom, with curious facial expressions, wondered where the strangers had come from. However, they would be similarly astonished by the speed at which the "uninvited guests" devoured the food and fluids that were soon afterwards placed before them.

It was some-time later, rumoured among the passengers, that the unknown men were stowaways and that they had been discovered hiding in the ship's engine room. But the Captain had allegedly acted with compassion after interviewing them in turn and listening to their individual stories of hardship, deprivation and dream of a better life. He decided that the men should be given the opportunity of earning a fair wage in London and they were placed in a vacant low-cost cabin, given entitlement to food and allowed the freedom to participate in all activities that were available to paid-up third-class passengers for the remainder of the trip.

The stowaways would have no difficulty merging with the rest of the passengers as they were found to be regular good guys. Furthermore, many individuals were able empathise with the circumstances that led to the young men's decision to enter the ship un-lawfully, and considered themselves fortunate to have received financial assistance for funding their own trip. Consequently, they could not, in all conscious, separate themselves from the stowaways as they too had been fleeing poverty and seizing the opportunity of a better life for themselves and family.

The incident relating to the stowaways had nonetheless become an interesting topic of debate and inter-discussion between separate cliques of passengers, and the catalyst for reaching out and forming friendships with others.

Getting Into The Swing

When men and women of different ages and marital status come together in a closed holiday environment, caution may be thrown to the wind as individuals crave the excitement of romance. Consequently, in an age when men from Caribbean cultures were expected to "make the first move", a large number of the species may have already been discretely "eying-up" the "talent", as lustful inclinations took hold. It had been for many, and in particular those from disadvantaged backgrounds whose lives had consisted mainly of sacrifice and toil, the very first time they had felt so liberated. They were now in a place where there was no work and plenty of play, and fully embraced what may have been for them all the once-in-a-life-time chance to just "let go" and have a good time.

What better place than the dancefloor to start things moving. And men who were at one time indecisive when it came to asking unknown ladies to accompany them in a dance, fearing rejection, found that their confidence had been boosted as a result of the discussions that had occurred across different groups in relation to the "sensational" revelation that stowaways had been discovered. As a consequence, these individuals now found no problem with boldly approaching and coming together with an attractive young lady of choice. On the other hand, many women attended these events for the purpose of having a good time, and would have, at any time, fall willingly into outstretched arms, and in unison with an equally enthusiastic partner, step to the beat of driving or smooth instrumental melodies being played by musicians that were recognised to be specific members of the ship's crew.

As the days flew by, it became commonplace that newly formed twosomes would be spotted engaging with each other in a variety of joint activities. And no-one blinked an eye when young men openly linked up with older women, or individuals who were allegedly married but un-accompanied by their spouse, got together with singletons. It was also not uncommon that these unlikely pairings may seek to spend private time together at any opportune moment during the day, or very likely following an evening of partying.

Oblivious to the ongoing shenanigans of her cargo of merry-makers, the liner maintained a steady pace and rode the waves through all weather patterns, including rough winds, heavy rain and hostile currents, as it headed across the Atlantic and onto its final destination. But even though passengers may have on occasions experienced an unsteady sensation under-foot whenever the vessel glided over turbulent seas, concerns in relation to safety issues seemed largely non-existent as the good-timers wallowed within their bubble of fun. Indeed, the carefree, self-indulgent and fun-packed environment of the ship may have led to some individuals having to pinch themselves to make sure that it was not just a beautiful dream. Or that they had died and gone to heaven. In reality, however, this particular cargo of West Indian passengers had never previously had it so good, but in thanks- giving to their "good fortune" endeavoured to attend the Christian Service that was held on the vessel every Sunday morning.

Discord And Altercation

As the journey progressed and individuals from the different Caribbean islands became increasingly integrated, there would be the occasional teasing relating to separate dialects or patois that were not at all times clearly understood or accurately interpreted. Although these language difficulties were not in general considered an issue, it was, for the minority, a trigger for mockery, ridicule or joke-making. Nonetheless, what may have been thought of as harmless taunting by the perpetrators, got out of hand at the bar after supper one night.

An alcohol-fuelled argument regarding the rights and wrongs of the spoken word led to physical retaliation by a target who felt that he had had enough. But what began as a fist-fight between two individuals, erupted into a free-for-all drunken brawl as men from opposing sides lashed out in defence of their own. It became a scene that depicted bodies wrestling on the floor and horrified women crouched in corners and screaming in fear. "Stop it! Stop it!" they pleaded. But crew members did not hesitate in their response, and were being assisted by various passengers in their efforts to bring about an end to the fracas. The situation was eventually calmed, but an overall sense of relief prevailed when it became clear that, apart from a few with minor cuts or bruises, no-one had sustained serious injury.

The majority of those who witnessed or may have been involved in the scrum, volunteered assistance with clearing any litter or reorganising dis-arranged furniture, prior to resuming separate activities. However, the alarming incident was for some-time thereafter the main topic of conversation or exaggerated rumour among the various passengers.

An Unlikely Pairing

Among the individuals that were caught up in discussing the altercation that occurred in the vicinity of the bar were Agatha and Alfonso, who found themselves standing next to each other when it was all over. "Da was jes like a fight yuh duz see in a salon in dem cowboy and Indian films," commented Alfonso.

"Yuh dam right," said Agatha.

"Yuh like Western films?" asked Alfonso.

"Yeh, man. Dats me favourite kinda movie," replied Agatha.

Having discovered a common interest, the couple entered into prolonged dialogue about the separate and shared "Cowboy and Indian" films they had seen in the cinema, their favourite "film stars", and with fervour recalled thrilling and exciting scenes that were depicted in the "once-upon-a-time" American Wild West that incorporated saloons, sheriffs, tense shoot-outs and cowboys on horseback firing their guns as they chased the bad guys. It was for them both an exhilarating coming together of minds, but neither Agatha nor Alfonso were aware that their shared interest in Western movies had signalled the beginning of a magical liaison. "How about meeting up again tomorrow?" suggested Alfonso, at the end of their riveting conversation.

"Call it a date!" replied Agatha, cheerfully.

After parting from Alfonso, Agatha felt that she had been floating on air as she made her way back to the shared cabin. She was so happy and couldn't believe that the dashing young "stud" Alfonso, desired to spend more exclusive time with her. Agatha couldn't help but feel flattered, and wondered why he would be attracted to her. After all, she was no longer a "spring chicken", and there were so many younger women he was able to choose from. But on coming to the decision that she would, in any case, go along for the ride, Agatha could not wait to tell her cabin-mates that Alfonso had asked to meet her the following afternoon. She was, however, disappointed that her exciting news did not receive the anticipated enthused response. But Sheila, Melrose and Olive seemed to be collectively unfazed as they looked at each other with knowing expressions which suggested that they were not particularly surprised. Indeed, they had already shared the opinion that the unlikely pair – Alfonso, the unattached desirable young man in his early twenties, and Agatha, an attractive happily married woman in her mid-thirties en route to join her husband in London – had clicked from the very beginning.

Having picked up on her friends' thinking, Agatha shrugged her shoulders and, in matter-of-fact fashion, insisted that Alfonso could never be anything more than a friend. Yes, she agreed to meet up with him; but no, it was nothing serious. The cabin-mates responded with a nod of the head, accompanied by the comment, "We'll see", before bursting into spontaneous laughter. Agatha knew well that the ladies were not convinced, but was nonetheless determined to keep her date with Alfonso. Moreover, she was actually looking forward to it!

The following afternoon, Melrose, Olive and Sheila made a point to be present in their shared cabin while Agatha readied herself for her very first date with Alfonso. The ladies were stunned by the transformation that occurred when Agatha had completed styling her hair and applying her make-up. As she beamed at them all with powdered face, highlighted by bright red lipstick and matching cheeks, the women could not help but express their admiration. "Yuh looking well nice," commented Sheila. "Thanks!" replied Agatha who could not help but being buoyed by the much-appreciated comment. "Ar go see all yuh later!" she exclaimed, as she cheerfully bounced out of the cabin and disappeared from view.

On arrival at their meeting point, Agatha was thrilled to find that Alfonso was already there and waiting. She immediately considered him a gentleman for not keeping her waiting. She was also impressed by how handsome he looked in his casual but snazzy attire. Alfonso appeared in an open-neck white shirt that was neatly tucked into a pair of slim-fitting blue trousers and accessorised with a fashionable silver-buckled black belt. "Gosh! Didn't realise he was so cute!" Agatha may have thought while trying to conceal being all of a sudden overtaken by a bubbling sensation in her stomach. Alfonso, on the other hand, immediately stepped forward with a friendly greeting, but he could hardly hide his admiration as he briefly cast his eyes over the bright red dress that defined her tiny waist and accentuated her ample bosom. "Ar like yuh dress." Said Alfonso in flattering tones. "Thank you," replied Agatha coyly, while attempting to impress him further with a red-lipped dazzling smile, which was immediately reciprocated with an equally mesmerising flash of golden teeth from Alfonso.

The couple had no idea how their date would proceed, but decided against participating in any of the various available activities. However, they enjoyed being in each other's company, and simply being able to spend quality time together may have been the intention. They walked leisurely around the decks of the ship, visited the bar, relaxed into chairs and maintained an interesting flow of conversation. It had been for them both a satisfyingly pleasant period of togetherness that served to reinforce an undeniable connection between them. But the hours flew by for Alfonso and Agatha, and it seemed that only a few minutes had passed when the call went out that supper was being served to "West Indian passengers".

"Fancy de dance tonite?" asked Alfonso.

"Yeh. Why not," replied Agatha.

"Good. Ar go catch-up with yuh later," assured Alfonso.

As a result of the new friendships that were being developed between individuals from the different established groups, there were those who may cross over and sit with others at meal times. And included the male members of the circle of friends, who did not always join their female counterparts at dinner. But cabin-mates Melrose, Olive, Sheila and Agatha were not persuaded to deviate from the custom of dining together, and very much looked forward to their light-hearted exchanges during a hearty meal and over a glass or two of wine. The women were, however, somewhat perplexed by Agatha's heightened sparkling persona when she eventually arrived following her rendezvous with Alfonso. But despite being repeatedly questioned about the time spent with her date by the curiously minded girlfriends,

Agatha refused to budge from her stance that the pair did nothing more than engage with each other while drinking at the bar. She failed to reveal that Alfonso had asked her to accompany him to an organised social event that very evening. Consequently, his unexpected appearance when everyone had finished eating, followed by Agatha's sudden announcement that she would see them all later, the women left behind, were speechless as they watched in amazement as Agatha strolled confidently with her date by her side, without even a backward glance!

On regaining their composure, the abandoned cabin-mates reflected on the fact that their initial recognition of a spark between Alfonso and Agatha had most likely become the reality. Even so, it was unanimously concluded that the couple should enjoy each other's company, if they so wished. After all, everyone seemed to be having a good time, so "good luck to them" would have been the collective sentiment that was very likely tinged with a tiny pinch of envy. However, only 26-year-old Olive was open in expressing her innermost feelings by vowing to resist temptation an remain loyal to her fiancé who was already residing in London and eagerly awaiting her arrival.

Meanwhile, Agatha and Alfonso had made their way to the entertainment lounge and wasted little time before getting into the swing of things. They joined in with other revellers on the dancefloor, and with beaming smiles gyrated energetically to the beat of the playing band. It was without doubt the highlight of their time spent together, thus far. And it was in care-free spirit that Agatha squealed with pleasure as Alfonso spun her around but she may not have noticed how his eyes twinkled with delight as a pair of shapely thighs were being repeatedly revealed beneath her twirling skirt. It was the occasion at which the unlikely pair would discover that they had a lot more in common than just an interest in "Cowboy and Indian" films. Neither could ignore the chemistry that was being ignited between them while merrily bopping to up-beat rhythms.

As the evening wore on, and softer music was being played, the couple wrapped their arms around each other and swayed blissfully to a series of melodic sounds. Not surprisingly, Agatha did not hesitate in agreeing to Alfonso's suggestion that they should take some time out for a little fresh air. Upon arrival at a secluded area on the lower deck, the couple fell spontaneously into a passionate embrace, and before too long Agatha was being led by the hand to Alfonso's cabin. He may have been aware that his cabin-mates were at the time involved in activities elsewhere and that their shared cabin would be unoccupied and available for enjoying a little private time with Agatha.

It was indeed a highly charged interlude for Agatha and Alfonso as they eagerly surrendered themselves fully to the hot and steamy pleasures of the flesh subsequent to entering the cabin. But the raunchy experience would result in Agatha being convinced that she knew exactly why Alfonso had so many girlfriends, having concluded that, "She who feels it, knows it well." And it felt good! Agatha was however miffed upon realising that her lover had fallen asleep when her ears were being penetrated by his snores. She knew then, that it was time to make her exit and reluctantly left his side and made her way to her cabin. Agatha was relieved to find that the girls were already in bed and consequently would not be subjected to any curious questioning relating to her relationship with Alfonso. Thank God, mumbled Agatha before quickly getting undressed and quietly climbing into her bunk-bed where she immediately fell into contented unconsciousness.

Following a restful night, Agatha felt rejuvenated upon awakening to a new day. She glowed with a feeling of well-being and with a smile that went from ear to ear, she stretched her limbs across the length and breadth of her bunk, sighed deeply and contentedly, before bursting into song. The ladies who were also awake, were flabbergasted; they had not known Agatha to be joyful so early in the morning, but she was now acting like the "cat with the cream."

"Like yuh had a good time last night?" queried Melrose.

"Me?" replied Agatha, admitting only to have enjoyed the dance.

"Yuh sure da was the only ting yuh enjoy last night?" quizzed Melrose in dubious tones that sparked fits of giggles among the sceptical women. But Agatha continued to hold her ground and stubbornly refused to elaborate on the matter. She was determined to keep her saucy secrets to herself for the time being, while savouring the amorous moments spent in her lover's arms. There would, however, be no turning back after their first romantic encounter. Agatha and Alfonso were unable to get enough of each other. The pair would continue to enjoy each other's company for the remainder of the journey. They shared a table at meal-times, discussed the movies, danced and made passionate love at every given opportunity.

However, while Alfonso remained care-free and void of any possible consequence to his holiday romance with an equally willing partner, Agatha, on the other hand, was occasionally overcome with feelings of guilt. Despite being a happily married woman en route to join her husband, she found that she was being irresistibly drawn to a man who made feel young and desirable. Agatha reasoned that even though her dalliance with Alfonso was undeniably erotic, it was nothing more than a short-term physical connection. Furthermore, she doubted that her husband would have acted any differently if the situation had been reversed.

Family Connection Uncovered

Although the holiday spirit that endured within the vessel had been conducive to romance and passionate liaisons, there was, nonetheless, a minority of people who chose to be involved in only platonic friendships. Among these individuals were the men who often engaged in robust conversations while loitering at the bar. Lionel, aged 40, who felt that he had been unceremoniously turfed out of the family home by being handed a one-way ticket to London, had been among those who enjoyed being in the company of other men. And it was during such moments of roguish banter with the boys that Lionel's attention was drawn to an attractive younger man whose appearance seemed vaguely familiar.

Even though the unknown individual to whom he was attracted, hung with a different group of men, Lionel no less felt compelled to make himself known to the stranger of interest. The younger man responded favourably to Lionel's friendly approach and self-introduction and reciprocated by shaking Lionel extended hand and revealing that he was called Clifford. When Lionel enquired into his country of origin, Clifford said that he was born on the island of St Lucia. "And am from Grenada!" declared Lionel.

"Grenada? Imagine that! My farder is Grenadian, too," chimed Clifford.

"Really! Yuh farder come from Grenada? Leh we talk. We must talk, boy!" urged Lionel.

On discovering the Grenada connection, the newly acquainted individuals decided to move onto a less noisy location for continuing a conversation that was felt to be of mutual interest. And still holding on to their glasses, the pair found a vacant table in a secluded area of the lounge and were comfortably seated before picking up on their conversation. Lionel was particularly interested to learn more about the family background of the man who vaguely resembled someone he knew or may have seen on the island of Grenada, but was unable to positively identify. Little did Lionel know that a shocking long-held secret was about to come into the light.

Clifford was quickly at ease in the presence of Lionel, who exuded nothing but warmth and friendliness, and, bolstered by alcohol, spoke freely and openly about his family back home. Lionel said that his Grenadian-born father, who was called Dickson, had been very much an absent "dad" who visited his mother, Darlene, and older brother, Lloyd, three or maybe four times each year. He went on to say that Dickson lived in his home country, Grenada, where he held a Senior Government position that involved meetings with Civil Servants based on various islands in the region.

It had been on one such visit that Dickson met Darlene, who had been employed as a receptionist at "The Ministry". The pair apparently formed a friendship and would arrange to socialise with each other whenever

Dickson visited St Lucia. The relationship was taken to the next level, and in time resulted in the birth of two baby boys. Darlene was hopeful that Dickson would one day relocate to St Lucia and that the boys would be raised by both parents in a happy family home, but it was not to be. Darlene's dreams were shattered when Dickson eventually confessed to having a wife and son back home in Grenada. Clifford went on to say that even though Darlene's hopes had been sorely dashed, she decided to carry on with the relationship, regardless. There was no change in the affectionate manner in which Dickson was welcomed whenever he appeared at the family home, and Darlene never failed to prepare his favourite meal.

Despite being unable to commit fully to his second family, Clifford swore that his father remained a reliable provider and showed interest the siblings' well-being and educational development. Dickson had been supportive of Clifford's decision to seek greater opportunities in the mother country and in particular his intention to enrol into one of London's Colleges for Further Education, with the end goal of obtaining teaching qualification.

Darlene's alleged experiences with Dickson would not normally have raised particular concerns. It was not uncommon in those days that seemingly happily married men also kept mistresses with whom they may produce additional siblings, commonly known as "outside children". However, whether based on the view that "half a loaf was better than none", deep-seated insecurities or acceptance of what could have been deemed their "lot in life", the "other woman" may, in some cases, remain loyal and submissive to the part-time lover who fathered her offspring.

Although Lionel had been aware of the cultural realities or accepted norms of the era, he was nonetheless astounded by Clifford's revelations. He had been joining-up the dots and everything fell into place. In particular, he now knew for sure, that the unidentified person who carried a resemblance of Clifford had all along been his very own father, Dickson. It had been for Lionel, a "mind-blowing" discovery that Dickson had not been everything he purported to be. The respected family man had been concealing a major secret. He was living a double life!

Clifford was similarly dumbfounded when Lionel announced that he (Lionel) was, without the slightest element of doubt, Dickson's Grenadian-born son and that they were, as consequence, half-brothers. "Really!" Gasped Clifford in astonishment. "Yes! Not a doubt in my mind." Replied Lionel. Both men fell silent and shook their heads as they reflected on their separate personal parental experiences with the man that fathered them both. But while still dazed by the remarkable coincidence, Lionel and Clifford would fall into each other's arms in a reciprocal warm embrace, and knock glasses in celebration of their remarkable discovery.

Unlike Clifford, who already knew of their father's indiscretions, Lionel had absolutely no clue, and consequently struggled with coming to terms with the skeleton that had unexpectedly popped out of the cupboard. Lionel decided against joining his friends for supper that evening and instead retired to bed and lay awake as thoughts of Dickson filled his head. As far back as Lionel was able to remember, Dickson had always been a dedicated family man with strong moral convictions. He was also an upstanding member of the local community, and considered a role-model for young men in the neighbourhood. But Lionel could not help but wonder whether his father had been having affairs with women who resided on islands other than St Lucia and with whom he may also have produced children.

Despite being troubled by the devastation that would be caused to his mother's perfect world, if the truth of her husband's betrayal should ever be leaked, Lionel felt compelled at this point to silently reflect on his own long-held secret. He had been throughout his adult life a closeted homosexual and had reached out to Clifford because of his appealing good looks, but was crushed when even the flimsiest hope of something more than friendship vanished when he discovered that the object of his desire was actually a very close relative.

Homosexuality was at that time culturally unacceptable and considered scandalous or sinful even, and Lionel was, as a consequence, terrified of bringing shame to his parents, or worse still, being disowned and banished from the family home. Moreover, being "queer" was in those days illegal, and buggery was a criminal offence punishable by at least ten years in prison. Nonetheless, an underground club consisting of same-sex membership was in existence, and sexual liaisons were being secretly pursued. But Lionel had for many years sustained satisfying relations with a man who presented as being happily married.

As a result of being haunted by his own personal demons, Lionel came to the conclusion that placing himself in the position of being "Judge and Jury" over his father's indiscretions would be highly hypocritical. And decided that it may be in everyone's best interests to just let "sleeping dogs lie".

FAMILY CONNECTION UNCOVERED

After a sleepless night of tossing and turning, caused mainly by the inability to switch off, totally, an overactive mind, Lionel prepared himself to face the new day before joining his friends at breakfast. Having not eaten the previous night, Lionel was ravenous and ignored comments being made by various members of the group as he tucked-in with relish to a meal which in his view was exceptionally good and very moreish. "How yuh eating so fast, boy?" "Take yuh time!" "Slow down!" they said.

At the end of breakfast, eyebrows were raised and heads turned as Lionel tapped on his stomach and burped loudly and unashamedly. But everyone's attention was all of a sudden diverted to the young man observed passing by, being warmly greeted by Lionel before he was introduced to the group as the newly discovered brother named Clifford. Needless to say, the introduction was met with collective exclamations of surprise that the men, who hailed from different islands, had by uncanny coincidence found each other on board a ship! And before too long, Clifford was being persuaded to grab a chair and join the clan at the breakfast table.

As the inquisitive conversations progressed, it became noticeable that Clifford had been making significant eye contact with the youngest among them, 19-year-old Sheila.

In subsequent days, it would become increasingly apparent that a close friendship was being formed between Clifford and Sheila. In particular, Sheila's cabin-mates were aware that she had been of late choosing to spend a significant amount of her time with her new friend. However, unlike Agatha, who had by this stage "owned up" to being in a relationship with Alfonso, and even bragged to her "envious" girlfriends about his amazing sexual prowess, Sheila remained largely silent. Despite being reluctant to discuss personal issues with her cabin-mates, Sheila may also have been a little uncertain of the exact nature of her relationship with Clifford. However, there was no doubt in her mind theirs had been a warm and friendly union, and that the couple looked forward to being together. Moreover, the fact that she was always in bed by 9pm at night was, in Sheila's view, proof that she had not been involved in any late-night "hanky-panky" with Clifford.

Although a significant number of passengers may have been involved in exciting "holiday romances," there were unions which went no further than flirtatious hugs and kisses, and may have included the association between Clifford and Sheila. Nevertheless, the members of the close circle of friends very much welcomed the affinity that had emerged between Clifford and Sheila, and wished them well. "They look so good together" being the unanimous complimentary observation. However, no one would have imagined that Lionel had been concealing his sexual ambiguity and that he craved an encounter with the man he desired but who was discovered to be his half-brother. It was, for Lionel, a bitter-sweet reality.

The fact that Lionel felt obliged to continue presenting his usually happy face and jovial disposition while experiencing profound emotional and mental torment could not be overstated. However, the need for keeping up appearances may also have been linked to being trapped in an euphoric bubble in which merry-making seemed to be the order of every day. Nevertheless, there would always be "exceptions to the rule" and individuals for reasons which may include an inability to fit-in, seemed resigned to be loitering on the side-lines. But even though Lionel had not been considered to be a loner, and was, on the contrary, an outgoing and flamboyant character with plenty of friends, he would, for a few short days, choose to stand on the fringe.

Fascinating Woman

Meanwhile, the high-flyer of the pack, 28-year-old Anthony, who revealed the seemingly unattainable aspiration of entering university, had been making waves with a sparkling young lady from Jamaica, known as Blossom. Unlike the majority of women within the specific culture of the era, Blossom's hair was not hot-pressed and curled. It was simply straightened and tied back in a ponytail. But her curvaceous figure, accentuated by a prominent "head-turner" derriere that shimmied when she walked, had been, for the majority of the red-blooded male passengers, tantalisingly seductive. And as a consequence, Anthony considered himself lucky to have "pulled" the hottest and most sought-after young lady on the boat. Even though he was undoubtedly the envy of his male contemporaries, the female members of his circle of close friends were horrified that a man from a privileged background, with a serious girlfriend back home, had, in their view, fallen for the charms of such an outlandish character.

It would appear that even though Anthony seemed sincere when he professed to have been missing his girlfriend, to whom he initially vowed to remain loyal, his focus was now being shifted towards Blossom. Anthony was captivated by her sensuality and gregarious personality, and in an environment that promoted self-fulfilment, she would become the object of his desires. Blossom, on the other hand, did not only admire Anthony's muscular physique but she was also being won over by his smiley face, twinkling eyes and humorous "joke a minute" banter. There could be no mistaking the mutual attraction that existed between them.

During the course of learning more about each other, Blossom revealed to Anthony that she was a 27-year-old single mother of two sons who supported her family by operating a seasonal fruit and vegetable market stall in her home village. And that when she was not selling her produce at market, provided a dress-making and hairdressing service to various women who lived within her local community.

Blossom went on to say that her sons had been placed in the care of their maternal grandmother and that she had arranged to stay with relatives who lived in Brixton, South London. But as Blossom paused for breath, Anthony quickly interjected by declaring that he, too, would be staying with friends who lived in Lewisham, which he believed was also located in South London. "That's good. Yuh never know, me and yuh might even bump into one another in the street one-a-dem days." Chirped Blossom in response.

"Hope so, but yuh mus give me yuh address, all the same," replied Anthony sheepishly, while wondering whether or not he may be moving a little too fast. But Blossom appeared undeterred. "Arrr-right!" she trumped cheerfully, before picking up on the conversation by adding that she dreamt of managing her very own hairdressing salon somewhere within the vicinity of South London at some-time in the future.

Even though Anthony may have considered Blossom's dream objective somewhat high-reaching for a woman of the time, he was, nonetheless, impressed by the totally unexpected disclosure. He would never have imagined that beneath the colourful exterior lay an ambitious, single-minded woman with a plan for achieving a higher standard of living for herself and her family. And as he reflected on the proverb that a book should not be "judged by the cover," Anthony began to see Blossom in a different light. The surprising reveal not only resulted in additional boxes being ticked, it also had the effect of enhancing Blossom physical appearance. She had become, in his view, even more sexy and desirable.

After listening intently to Blossom's account of her life so far, Anthony disclosed information regarding his own background including his dream of obtaining a university degree. Anthony added that he wanted to make his parents proud, as no one in the family had previously entered university. Blossom could hardly mask her admiration for a man who took her fancy, and wished him every success. She had been impressed by the fact that Anthony was not just hunky and very funny; he was also an educated man with high expectations.

Having spoken in relative depth to each other about their separate occupation and future aspirations, Blossom and Anthony had set the foundation for building a relationship. However, issues relating to past or on-going personal involvements would be cast aside as the twosome concentrated on the present and embraced the "here and now" by agreeing to be significant companions for the rest of the journey.

The couple looked forward to meeting up with each other on a regular daily basis and being involved in a variety of activities. However, Anthony could not help being slightly bemused on the occasion that Blossom appeared carrying a portable battery-operated record player in one hand and a vinyl record in the other. "Let us play some music today," suggested Blossom, before leading her willing companion into one of the smaller lounges, where the player was placed on a small table. Soon, Blossom had pointed the needle, attached to the arm of the player, carefully onto the vinyl, and Anthony was being blown over by the catchy sound that subsequently boomed across the room.

Suddenly, Blossom was on her feet. "Come on, Anthony, let's dance," she urged, as she bent forward and proceeded to swing her arms forward, backward, and from side to side, to the beat of thumping vocalised sounds, while singing in time with the chorus. "Ska! Ska! Ska! – Ska! Ska! Ska!" she repeated with considerable fervour, pausing only to beckon Anthony to her side. "Come on," she insisted. "Come on, man. Let's do it!" demanded Blossom, while forcefully pulling Anthony onto his feet. How could he resist, when sitting still had been without doubt the greater of the two challenges he was now facing. But to Anthony's surprise, after only a few awkward movements, he had fallen into the groove of the dance.

"Da easy, man!" he exclaimed triumphantly, as he found himself step-confident in following Blossom's lead, and was soon accompanying her in song: "Ska! Ska! Ska! – Ska! Ska! Ska!" they chanted in unison and at the top of their voices. The pair could hardly contain their glee as they "let rip" to the thumping drive of the music. And the spark that ignited between them promised many more days of shared jollies to come.

Among the small number of passengers who had joined the party having heard the music, was a sporty-looking young man holding a vinyl close to his chest. The onlooker quickly stepped forward after Blossom's record had finished playing and after introducing himself as "Cuthbert", asked if he would be permitted to use the portable record player for playing his own vinyl. "No problem!" replied Blossom willingly.

It was with a happy and wide smile that the enthused individual began the process of playing his record. "I is a Trini" (Trinidadian), Cuthbert declared in bragging tones, "and when it comes to music, we is the boss! Listen to dis tune, he continued. It is a Trinidadian Calypso but let me show you people the latest dance. They call it de saga ting. Cuthbert proceeded to show off to those around him a variety of freestyle movements that were timed to the drum-beat of the song. "It ain't hard. Jes do what yuh feel like doing," he announced gleefully, as he lifted his arms, gyrated his hips, and rotated them way down low. Before too long, everyone present, including Blossom and Anthony, was strutting their stuff by doing their separate version of the "saga ting". And there was unanimous agreement that the boastful "Trini" had been right all along. The "saga ting" was, without doubt, a great dance.

The Calypso was originated in the Caribbean and may be reflective of specific cultural experiences or occurrences. The particular sound is also integral to the street festivity known as Carnival, due to the rousing good-time rhythms.

Blossom, Anthony and the rest of the "saga ting" revellers were just one of many different groups of passengers who were at the same time involved in separate pleasurable pursuits. It had been a buzzing environment that was for the most part, filled with people that radiated glowing faces, spoke in heightened tones and were regularly gripped by rapturous laughter. However, in parallel with those who were engaged in their preferred fun activity, there was no ceasing of the seemingly unending flow of people in groups or lone individuals, crossing paths on stairwells, or as they wormed their way through the various areas of the vessel. But amidst the overall hustle and bustle, crew members remained calm, approachable, friendly and helpful, and maintained a vigilant and visible presence. And all the while, the floating hotel continued its steady progress across the ocean.

No Ordinary Day

As the ship sailed further away from the Caribbean and deeper into the Atlantic, passengers awoke on a particular morning to find that the winds were blowing loudly and violently across the decks. The ocean was choppy and the vessel rocked as it was being lashed by huge forceful waves. It was generally assumed that the ship had been caught in a storm but various individuals prayed for calm as they wobbled unsteadily, while others shivered uncontrollably, complained of "feeling cold" and reached for additional layers of clothing. The first experience of chilly weather would be on reflection considered pleasantly refreshing when compared with the freezing winter temperatures that were yet to be experienced.

Those who anticipated being warmed or comforted even, after consuming a hot beverage, may have rejoiced on hearing the announcement that breakfast was being served to "West Indian" passengers. However, as tables around which individuals were seated shifted from one side to the next, in motion with the ship, the unsettling sensations resulted in some passengers being nauseous and unable to digest nothing but a few sips of their preferred liquid. Others conquered their anxiety by bursting into song. But the robust among them whose appetites were not being impacted, enjoyed the ride, and they squealed with delight while sliding steeply in synch with the rocking ship.

In spite of the different responses, there could be no denying that everyone was relieved when the storm eventually subsided, and consequent to the return of calm, individuals wasted little time in engaging in separate everyday pleasurable routines.

As the humdrum of activity increased, passengers were suddenly alarmed on realising that what had been initially thought to be high-spirited screeches were, in fact, desperate screams for help that seemed to be coming from the vicinity of the pool. Anthony and Blossom who had been enjoying a leisurely stroll, were among concerned individuals who initially hurried to the location. And everyone present, including the couple, were shocked to be witnessing a fully-clothe young man with blood pouring from his head being pulled out of the water by members of the ship's crew, who had been maintaining a watchful eye at the pool-side.

After carefully positioning the unconscious injured man onto the floor, the responders wasted no time in initiating resuscitation. But within a few short minutes, the task was being taken over by fully equipped professional medics who, on receiving the alert, dashed to the emergency. At the same time, inquisitive bystanders were being held back by the crew as they surged forward and attempted a close-up view of the continuing operation. Anthony and Blossom continued their observation from a safe distance but were particularly shaken upon recognising the rescued person. He was, to their surprise, no other than Cuthbert, the "saga ting man." It seemed unbelievable to them both that the young "Trini", who had recently been so full of the joys of life, could now be lying at death's door. The pair were shaken to the core, but like other onlookers, held their breath and prayed for a favourable outcome.

There was a collective sigh of relief and everyone who prayed, felt that their prayers had been answered when, after many minutes of medical intervention, the patient coughed, spluttered, turned his head from one side to the next, and groaned. He was at that point lifted on to a stretcher and taken to the "sick bay" for follow-up treatment. And the usual noisy environment was now replaced by hushed but sobering verbal reflections on the "close shave" occurrence at the pool.

Blossom and Anthony had been particularly affected by the incident and were starkly awakened to the reality that nothing in life could be guaranteed. They would, as a consequence, decide to make the most of every minute spared by consummating their union in an explosion of impassioned embraces.

Lionel who had been haunted by issues that related to his personal life, was also among those who may have changed their outlook on life following the drama that unfolded at the pool. He had been reminded that life was short and unpredictable and that he should pull himself together, count his blessings and move on. Having decided to let go of his troubles, Lionel returned to being his old self. He was by nature, a vibrant and colourful character who brightened everyone's day.

It was later revealed that Cuthbert had been feeling a little disorientated following the storm, and that he suddenly slipped and stumbled while walking beside pool. He was unfortunately knocked unconscious upon falling, head first into water.

The Return Of The Good Times

There was an overall sense of relief and everyone appeared delighted when the injured man had fully recovered and was discharged from the treatment bay. It hailed the return of the good times for those who had refrained from participating in fun activities while the fate of their fellow passenger remained uncertain. And included a rejuvenated Lionel, who in spite of being a "fully paid up" member of the circle of friends, loved hanging out with "the boys", or like-minded men who enjoyed being in each other's company. It had been a forum where the men felt uninhibited and free to drink and smoke as much as they liked, discuss the popular game of cricket, talk dirty or brag about actual or imagined, past sexual encounters with particular members of the opposite sex. But there were also a significant number of female passengers, who like some of their male counterparts, decided against being involved in holiday romances, and simply enjoyed gossiping with other girls.

Evening cabaret presentations by the ship's musicians and entertainers who were also members of the crew, had also been popular events attended by many passengers. But party-goers were also encouraged to attend or take part in the various competitions that were being organised for passenger participation only, and included singing, dance and fancy-dress contests. And when it was announced at the end of a particular show, that interested passengers were being invited to compete in a Fancy-Dress Competition on a specified evening, the invitation sparked the imagination of Lionel, who was at the time, among the audience.

Thereafter, Lionel could think of nothing else. He felt that the competition would be a platform for showing off to others a different side to his personality. For as long as he could remember, Lionel carried a secret fetish for dressing in women's clothing, which may occur, albeit underground, with one or possibly two individuals of similar persuasion. But any indulgence in his guilty pleasure would often be accompanied by fits of giggles as he imagined the shock and horror expressions on his parents' faces if they were able to see what he had been really getting up to on occasions when their one and only son was supposed to be spending an innocent social evening with friends.

Lionel had an idea. He decided that his best option would be to enter the competition disguised as a nursing officer, and on request, acquired a large garment from a bemused but compliant female member of the medical team after he had informed her of his plan. "Hope it will be a good enough fit for you – it's the largest one I was able to find," said the woman. "Oh, by the way," she added with chuckle in her voice. "Thought this might come in handy." And Lionel was pleasantly surprised that he had been given a tube of purple lipstick. "Thank you! Thank you!" he repeated excitedly, before hurrying off to his cabin.

In the privacy of his bathroom Lionel proceeded to squeeze himself into the white dress that had been loaned to him by the kindly medic. However, even though it clung tightly around his large frame and was not long enough to cover his knees, Lionel could not help but feel gloriously feminine as he posed and twirled in front of the bathroom mirror and ran his hands smoothly along his stomach and around his hips. It was for him a precious moment of fulfilment.

After undressing and getting back into his regular clothing, Lionel carefully folded the garment and concealed it beneath the mattress of his bunk-bed. He decided that his planned entry into the competition should not be revealed to his friends until the actual day of the event.

The Outsiders

Meanwhile, the gleeful atmosphere persisted as passengers focused on having the best time ever. Even so, there were individuals, including a few members of the circle of friends that were unable to get into the party mood and remained somewhat detached from the majority.

Melrose, aged 43, who was fleeing an abusive husband, continued to be gripped by feelings of uncertainty. She had, for over twenty years, endured an existence in which she was being emotionally and psychologically abused by a domineering and controlling spouse. But although she had escaped her torturous life and was now on her way to a new beginning, Melrose self-confidence remained in tatters. Moreover, she worried constantly about the wellbeing of the siblings left behind; but Melrose also feared that the abandoned husband, may at some point in the future, reappear and take her back home. Consequently, while cabin-mate Sheila was being happily involved with Clifford and likewise, Agatha with Alfonso. Melrose would spend a large amount of time in company with 26-year-old Olive, who, in contrast, had been looking forward, with considerable excitement, to a rosy future with the man she was planning to marry.

Olive, an attractive and vivacious woman, had declined a number of approaches from men who would have liked to develop a personal relationship with the attractive young lady. But Olive had been determined to remain loyal to her fiancé, John, who was already in London and anxiously awaiting her arrival. Despite appearing starry-eyed and being in the throes of a new romance, the relationship between Olive and John had, in reality, been long-standing. The pair were raised in the same town community, attended the local elementary school and were childhood sweethearts. Both sets of families approved of their union and were delighted when, after arriving in London two years previously, John had demonstrated honourable intentions by accumulating, from his earnings as a bus conductor, the funds required for purchasing the ticket that would enable Olive to join him in London.

Olive felt that her heart would burst with intense feelings of bliss whenever she thought of being once again in the arms of her fiancé. She believed whole-heartedly that they were destined to be together, and were without doubt each other's soul-mate. Olive loved nothing better than being alone in her cabin, where she would snuggle into her bunk-bed and drift into daydreaming about marrying her beloved, and thereafter sharing a happy life with him. But Olive's experiences on the journey, and her thoughts, feelings and emotions were being documented in the letters she wrote to John on a daily basis. Each letter would be neatly folded on completion and slotted within the pages of a book that was secured beneath her pillow. It had been Olive's intention to present them to John as testament of her devotion at an appropriate moment subsequent to their reunion.

The second-best thing for Olive was spending quality time with Melrose, who was at all times a enthusiastic listener, and to whom she could freely gush her romantic thoughts and fairy-tale expectations. But Melrose would be cheered, or entranced even, by Olive's outpourings of joy. Moreover, her spirit was uplifted from being touched by the aura of happiness that surrounded her "lucky" friend, Olive. And Melrose would temporarily put to one side her personal woes and insecurities.

Melrose was overcome with emotion when out of the blue one day, Olive handed her a sheet of paper on which the contact details of her fiancé, John, had been written. "Here, take this and make sure yuh send me your address so that I could invite yuh to me wedding," said Olive with a smile. The much appreciated gesture had been a token of the close friendship between the women that was expected to continue long after they had settled into new lives somewhere in London.

Meanwhile, Lionel had been becoming increasingly excited by thoughts of the forthcoming Fancy Dress Competition, and, bursting with anticipation, was no longer able to withhold his intentions from all of his close friends, and decided to reveal his plan to cabin-mate Gilbert. Despite being a loner and a man of few words, Gilbert was nonetheless considered to be the most trustworthy member of the circle.

Gilbert was a pleasant but quiet and reserved individual, but, similar to Olive and Melrose, displayed little interest in attaching himself to any particular person outside of the group. Consequently, when his thrill-seeking cabin-mates were occupied with their separate pleasurable pursuits, Gilbert remained a permanent member of the "lonely club" and a solitary soul who spent much of his time leaning over the deck of the ship and staring into the ocean, while drawing deeply on a cigarette. Gilbert worried about the future, and the pitfalls that he may have to overcome during his quest for a better life. Despite being hopeful that the glowing stories rumoured about "life in London" were correct, he was at the same time somewhat apprehensive about the unknown. It was, in Gilbert's view, all too good to be true, and he envisaged difficulties ahead. He wondered whether he would ever realise his dream of a better life for himself and family back home.

Having Fun At The Competitions

Lionel's disclosure to Gilbert regarding his intention to enter the upcoming Fancy Dress Competition, dressed in a nurse's uniform, was met initially with a spontaneous outburst of laughter. However, after pausing for breath and regaining his composure, Gilbert slapped Lionel on the back and applauded him for having the courage required for prancing around in front of an audience in women's attire. "Yuh go bring de house down. Believe me!" exclaimed Gilbert in reassuring tones. But even though Lionel had been shored-up by his friend's words of encouragement, he insisted that the decision to enter the contest was intended as a surprise, and should therefore be kept confidential.

Despite pledging to remain silent, Gilbert was compelled to share the juicy information with at least one other within the circle. But the spillage resulted in every member of the group having knowledge of Lionel's plan to participate in the up-coming competition. The disclosure triggered a tirade of humorous assertions and situations that involved imagined effeminate imitations of Lionel, dressed in women's clothing, "strutting his stuff" in front of an audience. But after the joke-making and laughter had been exhausted, it was generally agreed that the show should not be missed, and that every member of the group, including Olive, would support their friend,

Lionel, by being present at the event and ensuring that he is loudly and enthusiastically applauded.

Time flew swiftly by, and suddenly the day and time scheduled for the Fancy Dress Competition had arrived. And it was to a background of calypso music blasting from the juke-box that a fairly large number of passengers bopped into the party lounge and towards separate chairs, on which the jiggling would continue. Everyone appeared to be in jolly mood as they waited in anticipation of being entertained by a variety of "idiots" clad in comical costumes. No one seemed to know exactly who the contestants would be, but the circle of friends who were present in force and sat closely together could think of nothing but Lionel's appearance. They fidgeted in their seats as they waited anxiously for the show to begin and, in particular, to hear the name "Lionel" being called to the stage.

Suddenly, a member of the crew appeared and announced that the competition was about to start. He went on to say that following the appearance of all the contestants, they would be returned to the forum and the audience would be required to applaud each competitor in turn, and the person who receives the loudest cheers would be declared the winner. The statement was concluded with the audience being urged to relax and enjoy the show.

Everyone clapped, cheered and shrieked with laughter as, one by one, the contestants appeared and, after parading their costumes, went on to impersonate their particular character. The line-up included a one-eyed pirate bellowing "Hi-ho, Silver". A sparsely dressed tribal warrior with brightly painted chest, matched with colourful head-band and loin-cloth, who waved a stick while performing a "war dance". There was also the "Market Trader", dressed in heavily layered skirts with a basket of fruit precariously placed on her head and bellowing "Ripe mangoes for sale! Get your mangoes here!" But the lounge erupted into hysterical laughed when the "Market Trader" unexpectedly tripped on her skirt and fell flat on her face.

The already uproarious atmosphere went up a gear and burst into "ear-numbing" thunderous applause when Lionel stepped onto the stage wearing his ill-fitting white dress. The bodice of the garment clung tightly to a bustline that appeared to have been stuffed with an indeterminable number of odd socks. The skirt fell above his knees and exposed a pair of hairy legs. But the audience was also captivated by Lionel's larger-than-life flamboyant presence. He seemed to be in his element as he focused on playing the role of a bizarre, sexy nurse. With both hands planted on his hips, Lionel twisted and turned, pouted his brightly painted red lips, cocked his head to one side, and proceeded to swing his hips in an exaggerated "glam-girl" fashion while prancing across the stage in a pair of large shoes. The highly comical performance ended with a standing ovation and a torrent of wolf whistling.

The two acts that followed, paled by comparison with Lionel's electrifying performance and, as a result, received only lukewarm responses from the spectators.

After all the contestants had showcased their unique talent, they were, as everyone expected, returned to the stage for the judging. The people were required to applaud as loudly as possible for the individually named act. But although the friendship group planned to increase

Lionel's chance of winning the competition by "raising the roof" in a surge of noisy support, it had been suggested by the overwhelming tumultuous response he received when his name was called, that the majority also backed their man. It was consequently generally assumed that Lionel would be triumphant on the night. However, when it was eventually confirmed that he had indeed won the competition, the announcement was greeted with an explosion of claps of approval, wild cheering and the stomping of feet.

Lionel beamed with pleasure as he stood at the front and soaked up what was for him the most amazing few moments of his life. He had exhibited to a fairly large number of people a side to his personality that was previously revealed to just a few like-minded men who resided in his home country. But above all, this particular audience indicated that they absolutely loved him!

Bolstered by his newly found fame and resulting feelings of self-assurance, Lionel would eventually saunter from the stage with a pronounced bounce that ignited a greater amount of whistling and hilarious comments. "Never yet seen any woman shake bam-bam like that man!" exclaimed an individual in a voice that could be clearly heard above the rest. It had been, for Lionel, the actual "icing on the cake". He was elated to have received what was, in his view, the best compliment imaginable.

After quickly getting back into his regular clothing and wiping the make-up from his face, Lionel joined his friends, who had been patiently awaiting his presence. He was greeted by repetitive well-intentioned but hefty back-slaps, accompanied by congratulatory declarations such as "Well done!" or "Yuh done well, boy!"

"Aright! Aright! Spear me back," pleaded Lionel, while momentarily stepping away from the group. But within seconds the celebration was being "kicked off" by everyone raising their glass in honour of the new celebrity within their midst. It was for them all a most joyous occasion.

The following morning, when Melrose was taking her daily walk around the deck, she heard a familiar voice. "Melrose!" She looked back to find Gilbert hurrying towards her. "You want company?" "Be my guest," replied Melrose enthusiastically. Although the various members of their group had separate connections with particular individuals of interest, or may have aligned themselves with individuals who shared similar interests, Gilbert and Melrose were solitary souls who spent much of their time in deep personal thoughts about the future. Melrose had been apprehensive about the prospect of independently starting afresh in a foreign land while Gilbert struggled with a nagging sense of foreboding that the streets of London were not paved with gold as rumoured, and anticipated difficulties ahead.

The coming together of Gilbert and Melrose during a walk along the upper deck would herald the beginning of a valued platonic friendship. Although there was no chemistry between them, Gilbert and Melrose were able to communicate freely and openly, and were empathetic to each other's expressed uncertainties regarding the future.

Following the popularity of the Fancy Dress Competition, two further contests were organised, and the circle of friends, including Olive, made a point of being at each event. Olive, who was initially determined to steer clear of all organised social functions, discovered her liking for that particular form of entertainment after being present at the Fancy Dress Competition in support of Lionel. It had been so much fun, and she decided there and then that she would continue attending similar shows.

The Dance Competition was yet another popular event. Each contestant was egged on by the crowd. "Come on, boy. Do yuh ting," they chanted, while imitating particular hand, foot and body movements. But expressions of surprise were quickly followed by a chorus of enthusiastic applause when Cuthbert, clothed in white tee-shirt and blue jeans, leapt forward and proceeded to gyrate to the rhythm of the music. No one expected that Cuthbert would have entered the contest so soon after recovering from injuries sustained at the pool. Nonetheless, he appeared fit and lithe as he twisted, turned and shuffled his feet to the "saga ting" groove. The crowd went wild, and there were no surprises that, by popular vote, Cuthbert was declared winner of the competition. He was subsequently crowned undisputed "King of Dance" by his fellow passengers.

The circle of friends was very much looking forward to being present at the Singing Contest that was scheduled to take place the following day. But when they were informed by Anthony that his girlfriend, Blossom, would be taking part in the competition, they decided that they would noisily support her performance regardless of whether or not it was deserved.

On the evening of the event at which Blossom was expected to be participating, the group was among others who entered the designated lounge, sat on available chairs and waited in anticipation for the entertainment to begin. Before too long, the presenter of the show came onto the raised platform at the front of the lounge. She explained to the audience that similar to previously held competitions, the contestants would be judged in accordance with the length and volume of applause being given to each performer at the end of the show. The named competitors were in turn subsequently called to the stage and invited to deliver their song.

The first contender was greeted with polite hand-clapping, but as he sang a much-loved Caribbean folk song of the day – "Yellow bird up high in banana tree. Yellow bird, you look all alone like me. Has your lady friend left the nest again? That is very sad, make me feel so bad…. The audience realised that he had been singing out of tune and booed him off the stage.

The rendition of another well-known ditty delivered in high-pitched but tuneless tones by the second contestant was also subjected to a barrage of merciless mockery.

After halting the first too acts that were generally considered to be "not good enough" the audience gleefully anticipated ridiculing yet another untalented contestant. But they would be unexpectedly but pleasantly surprised when a familiar face appeared and proceeded to deliver, in pitch-perfect tones, his very own version of a popular Jamaican melody of the era. And he was soon being accompanied by almost everyone at the show, in crooning the melodic chorus that was at the time so personally reflective of individual circumstances: "Sad to say am on my way, won't be back for many a day. My heart is down. My head is turning around. I had to leave a little girl in Kingston Town." The poignant performance was enjoyed by everyone at the show and ended amid wild cheers of approval.

The people were sitting calmly and pensively following a stirring performance that had without doubt rekindled memories of loved ones left behind. However, if the audience was hoping for yet another sing-along, they were not about to be disappointed. And when the young lady stood in front of them and proceeded to render the up-beat Trinidadian calypso of the time, many within the audience could not help but tap their feet while belting out well-known lyrics; "Jean and Dinah, Rosina and Clementina…"

Blossom, whose appearance was being eagerly awaited by the circle of friends, became the fifth contender to be introduced to the audience. However, in spite of the enthusiastic reception, various members of the group could not help but wonder if their effervescent friend would be able to better the last two acts. But Blossom, dressed in a low-cut, close-fitting red dress and wearing a pair of pointed white shoes, would immediately get into her groove. She radiated confidence and attitude, as she held her arms up high and moved slowly and seductively for a moment or two, before delving into what would be the most tantalizing performance of the competition. "Oh, Carolina. Oh, Carolina, Oh, Caroline from Jamaica, come on and …," She drawled suggestively. Although individuals of Jamaican heritage who were among the audience would have been familiar with the uniquely earthy and pulsating sound, others were captivated by the exciting "new music."

The audience had been "blown over" not only by Blossom's gutsy delivery of her song, but also the accompanying sultry dance. It was considered an all-together sensational performance and she was rewarded with a deafening standing ovation.

The judging may have been only a formality, as it seemed that everyone who witnessed Blossom's presentation felt that she was without doubt, the "big hit of the night". Consequently, there were no surprises that Blossom received an overwhelming response when the competition was being judged at the end of the show. She had overtaken all the other participants by becoming everyone's favourite competitor.

The audience was exhilarated at the end of the much enjoyed evening of entertainment. Moreover, Anthony was exceedingly proud that Blossom had snatched victory on the night. But thoughts of his girlfriend back home may not have been at the forefront of his mind as he held Blossom closely in a loving embrace, and reflected on being the luckiest man on the boat, having picked himself an extraordinary woman.

The different competitions that occurred during the throbbing carefree days at sea included those that were informally arranged between different groups of passengers. These may have involved various ball or board games and dominoes matches.

Tragedy Strikes

Although the passengers were fundamentally aware that the vessel had been maintaining a steady speed as it navigated the journey across the vast waters of the Atlantic, they may have lost track of the exact number of days they had been travelling on the high seas. However, keeping abreast of time may not have been the priority for individuals who were primarily focused on being active members of the ship community. Moreover, any initial suspicion that the surreal situation they had entered into was all too good to be true, and would probably be "short-lived", may have seemed a distant memory as they surrendered, happily and wholeheartedly, to the "here and now." And as a consequence, the likelihood of any obstruction to the status quo would not have been imagined.

The female members of the circle of friends who shared a cabin had not been overly concerned on the day that Olive complained of having a throbbing headache. However, when it was being accompanied by intermittent periods of vomiting, Melrose, Agatha and Sheila, were of the opinion that Olive's symptoms may have been linked to something she had eaten, and advised her to drink plenty of water. The ladies were pleased that Olive, who was laying quietly on her bed, had fallen into a snooze. "At least she is resting." said Melrose. "Yes." came the collective reply. They also shared the view that she would be "fine tomorrow," but subsequent to the call that supper was being served, the cabin-mates felt that Olive should not be roused and they set off for the evening meal without her.

After supper had been eaten, the girlfriends decided against participating in any of the evening's organised activity or even the usual after-dinner humorous exchanges, and with Olive in mind, hurried back to the cabin. They were relieved to find that she had been continuing to "sleep-off" the nauseous headache. "That is a good sign. She is having a well-deserved rest." Commented Melrose with conviction. "Yep! Exactly what the body need. She will be right as rain tomorrow," piped Agatha in reply. The reassuring prediction was met with as chorus of positive responses, and before too long the women had prepared themselves for bed and were quietly climbing into their separate bunk. They ensured that Olive remained undisturbed by continuing to communicate with each other in hushed voices prior to drifting into sleep.

On awakening the following morning, Melrose immediately checked on Olive, but was troubled to find that Olive, with whom she shared a bunk, had still not moved from her original position. She continued to lie peacefully on her back with her eyes tightly shut and her arms folded on her chest. Overcome with feelings of anxiety, Melrose reacted by forcefully shaking her friend. "Olive! Olive! Wake up! Wake up!" she yelled frantically.

"What happen? What happen?" cried Sheila and Agatha, having being suddenly jolted out of sleep by Melrose's screams.

"She won't wake up," replied Melrose in panicked tones.

"Oh, my God! Let me go and get help," said Agatha, and she rushed from the cabin dressed only in her nightgown. Within a few short minutes, Agatha had reappeared, accompanied by two members of the ship's crew, who immediately attended to Olive. They were also unable to achieve a response, and sought professional medical intervention. It was, however, to no avail and Olive was stretchered to the appropriate facility after relevant information had been obtained from those who had witnessed her deterioration.

Despite being assured by the medical team that they would be kept informed of Olive's progress, Agatha, Melrose and Sheila were nevertheless worryingly perplexed that what appeared to have been nothing more than a headache could have so quickly developed into a critical situation. "Let us say a prayer" suggested Melrose. And without uttering a word, the ladies responded by immediately falling onto their knees and together prayed for Olive's full and speedy recovery.

After the praying had ended, the anxious friends picked up on their daily routine by getting dressed and making their way to the breakfast-lounge. On arrival at their shared table, the male members of the group who were already seated, were immediately informed of Olive's condition. The unexpected disclosure was met with a great deal of concern and resulted in very little breakfast being consumed on the day. The normally effervescent gathering had become depressingly downbeat as everyone sat in silence and pondered over the possible outcome of the unexpected but mysterious ailment that had so suddenly befallen a much liked member of their circle.

Agatha, Melrose and Sheila eventually returned to their shared cabin and nervously awaited the promised update on Olive's progress. However, when a female member of the medical team later appeared accompanied by the Captain of the ship and also the Chaplain, the women were unable to ignore their sombre facial expressions and braced themselves for "grim news". They were dumbfounded and shaken to their very core when the apologetic Medical Officer confirmed their worst fears. The medic explained in softly spoken and sympathetic tones that health-care personnel had failed in their efforts to resuscitate the patient. The spokesperson went on to say that the ship was not equipped with the required resources for determining the exact cause of death, but the signs and symptoms reported by the women in relation to the onset of Olive's ill health, suggested that she had most likely suffered a bleed on the brain.

The ladies were afterwards informed by the Captain that a telegram had been wired to Olive's closest relatives, at the address registered, advising them of the tragic loss of their loved one and the related circumstances. At that point, Melrose, to whom Olive had revealed her hopes and dreams for the future, interjected with the suggestion that she should personally deliver the deceased's belongings to her grief stricken fiancé. Mindful of the fact that Melrose and Olive had been each other's confidante during the journey, Agatha and Sheila expressed no objection in relation to Melrose's request. The Captain and the Medical Officer also supported the proposal.

The Cleric finally delivered a few words of comfort to the women and offered a prayer in memory of the deceased. He also prayed for the surviving members of Olive's family and her closest friends.

Traumatised by the sudden and unexpected loss of a dear friend, the heartbroken ladies sat numb and reeling in shock and disbelief long after the important guests had exited their cabin. They struggled to fully absorb the reality of it all and may even have wondered whether they had all been trapped in a horrific nightmare.

Breath-taking view

Although what was initially assumed to be no more than a common headache had progressed into something more worrisome, the women had prayed diligently for Olive's full recovery. And despite their concern, harboured little doubt that she would bounce back to full health following treatment. She was, after all, just 26 years of age, fit, happy and full of life. Moreover, she was so looking forward to reuniting with her fiancé in London, and in particular to becoming his wife. The fact that Olive was, in the blink of an eye, no longer around, had not only been overwhelmingly crushing for the surviving cabin-mates, it had also re-ignited their awareness of the fragility of life.

The bombshell revelation of Olive's untimely demise had been a bolt from the blue. It sent shock waves throughout the ship and resulted in the seemingly forever glitzy hurly-burly environment being replaced by stillness and the mournful mutterings of dispirited souls.

A service, led by the ship's Pastor, was subsequently held in remembrance of the young life that had been cut so devastatingly short. The ceremony was attended by almost everyone on board the vessel and included the Captain, Medical Officers and crew members. The women with whom Olive had shared a cabin were later informed that on health and safety grounds, the body of their deceased friend, had been discreetly lowered into the ocean.

In spite of the tragedy that had profoundly impacted the ship's community and abruptly ruptured the bubble of fun, the vessel continued forging ahead as scheduled, and there were no changes in relation to the day-to-day operational procedures that were in place within the ship.

The Other Side Of The Ocean

Landmass spotted

Although time seemed to be flying by when a large number of passengers who had been gripped by the feel-good factor, involved themselves in pleasurable activities, the days seemed depressingly long and gloom-filled following the devastating passing of Olive. But hearts would be lifted on the clear, sunny day, that landmass was sighted on the horizon. It was subsequently reported that the ship had crossed over to the other side of the ocean and was sailing towards the Canary Islands. The passengers were delighted that they had at long last, arrived at the end stage of their journey.

After progressing steadily alongside the various islands, the ship eventually docked into port on the island of Tenerife. Passengers were told that Tenerife was the largest of the group of islands, and that they were being offered the opportunity of disembarking and enjoying a few hours on shore. The majority welcomed the freedom of being able to touch ground again after several weeks of being in a closed environment. Moreover, they were thrilled that they were being offered the "rare" opportunity of visiting an "exotic" place that was situated in a different hemisphere.

Subsequent to disembarking the ship, the circle of friends was one among the different groups of West Indian visitors that hung together as they strolled leisurely along the coastal promenades and streets beyond, while observing and commenting on the interesting surroundings. They would come across lines of traders with their various souvenirs and general merchandise on display, but even though there were those who may have wished to purchase specific items that had caught their eye, only a few possessed the necessary funds. Many, and in particular those from impoverished backgrounds, had already exhausted every dollar they owned on purchasing their ticket for the "once in a lifetime" dream trip to London, and were, as a consequence, penniless. Nonetheless, they very much appreciated being able to escape the confines of the ship and spend a little time simply exploring local areas on an exquisite island where they were being greeted at every juncture by locals with smiling faces.

Despite their underlying sadness, the passengers felt rejuvenated on re-boarding the vessel after an exhilarating few hours spent on the island of Tenerife. It had been the first time following the loss of Olive that anyone had felt so enlivened. Even so, there may have been those, and in particular the members of her circle of friends, who could not help but feel a little guilty for being so refreshed. However, the tide was beginning to turn and there would be no going back. And the enduring sombre environment would gradually evaporate as passengers became increasingly captivated by magnificent views of landscapes encountered as the vessel continued the course of the journey.

After emerging from the Strait of Gibraltar, the ship cruised along the coastline of Spain and docked into port at Barcelona, a city on the northern coast of the country. Although many passengers would have had knowledge of Spain and may even have heard about the Strait of Gibraltar, very few, if any, would have anticipated actually having the opportunity of casting eyes on those specific areas. These particular young West Indian travellers of the era had no idea that the journey to London would have taken them to places they may have learnt about in Geography classes at school or viewed on world maps. They never expected that they would one day actually visit these far-away areas of the globe. Consequently, everyone was elated when it was announced that the ship would remain in port at Barcelona for 24 hours, and that individuals were once again, free to disembark.

On entering Barcelona, the tourists were happy to find that the locals were equally as friendly and welcoming as the people that were previously encountered on the island of Tenerife. But they would also find themselves having to resist being approached by vendors in their attempt to dispose of some of the articles being displayed for sale. However, despite being unable to make purchases, due to lack of cash, the visitors were not deterred from stopping to admire the various displayed merchandise. These included not only souvenir trinkets but also large culturally dressed dolls, sunglasses, bags, cigarettes, cigars and packets of tobacco. However, the tourists' experience in Barcelona had been enriched simply by being able to wander freely around the town while wallowing in the glorious sunshine. And even though various groups of sight-seers may have lost direction and consequently had difficulty finding their way back to the ship, it was, nonetheless, an overall memorable adventure that was generally felt, at that time, to have been worth a lot more than money or material purchases.

After departing the shores of Spain, the vessel began voyaging towards Italy and its final port of destination. But even though the time spent crossing the Atlantic may have appeared to be largely a never-ending journey of pleasure, the day prior to leaving the ship for the very last time seemed to have all of a sudden arrived. However, the passengers looked forward with anticipation to the Captain's end-of-journey dinner and dance event, that was scheduled to take place that very evening.

In the meanwhile, the penultimate day at sea was generally spent packing suitcases in readiness for the final disembarking. It was, however, particularly harrowing for Melrose as she gathered Olive's possessions together with the intention of delivering them personally to the fiancé of her deceased dear friend. But Melrose was cheered by being convinced that Olive's heartfelt letters and diary entries would be gladly received and should provide much-needed comfort to the bereaved young man.

It had also been the day when contact details were being exchanged between individuals who wished to keep in touch subsequent to settling into new homes around the London area. And in particular between those who were significantly connected, such as Anthony and Blossom,

Sheila and Clifford, Melrose and Gilbert, and recently discovered half-brothers, Lionel and Clifford.

Despite being involved in an unprotected torrid affair, the connection between Agatha and Alfonso had been nothing more than an intense short-term holiday romance, and the couple had no intention of continuing their relationship beyond the journey. However, unbeknown to Alfonso, Agatha suspected that the symptoms she had been experiencing suggested that she may have fallen pregnant with her lover's child. But if it was indeed the case, abortion was not an option that Agatha was able to consider, and in the meanwhile thought only of reuniting with her husband, who was expected to welcome her arrival at London's Waterloo station.

The Final Hurrah

The fact that a large number of passengers, dressed in colourful party outfits, attended the Captain's dinner in spite of the unexpected tragic loss of Olive, may have been reflective of the collective resolve that each given day was precious and should be grabbed and lived to the fullest. But even though the lavish meal and accompanied free-flowing wine had been thoroughly enjoyed by everyone at the table, the members of the circle of friends were among the minority of individuals who in respect of the deceased, decided against participating in the partying that followed.

As the music trumped at the end of dinner, those who had anticipated ending the journey across the Atlantic with a bang, let loose and strutted their stuff to every tune played. The high-spirited party-goers ecstatically slid across the floor, hopped, bopped, leaped, twirled, jived and shuffled to the various rock and rhythm and blues hits of the day. Gyrated their hips in abandoned fashion and jumped to the calypso beat. Bent their bodies forward and marched in time with the pulsating base of the "Ska". Gleefully swung their arms and feet from side to side and twisted down low while bellowing, "Let's twist again, like we did last summer …." And stepped forward and backward, and from side to side in time with Latin rhythms.

The gloriously noisy rave continued until the early hours of the morning, when the giddy revellers returned to their respective cabins. The very last night of entertainment had been, for them all, the pinnacle of the good times spent on the vessel.

Unforgettable Journey Ends

The passengers were required to disembark with all of their belongings, for the last time, after the ship arrived at its final destination and docked into the port of Genoa in Italy. The English-speaking passengers on route to London were driven by coach to a hotel in the town of Genoa, where they stayed for two memorable days during which they took the opportunity of visiting local places of interest.

The travellers were thereafter transported by train to Calais where they boarded the Ferry that would carry them across the English Channel and onto Dover.

London Is The Place For Me

Upon arrival at Dover, the young West Indians were enamoured by their first sighting of the "White Cliffs of Dover" as referenced in the patriotic song that was loved by so many around the globe during World War 2. They were soon afterwards led towards a train station where they climbed into a train that was headed for London's Waterloo station, and were subsequently enthralled by passing views of the beautiful English countryside as the train speeded on its journey.

In spite of being acutely aware that one of their number was missing due the sad and unexpected passing of Olive, the new arrivals had been overwhelmed by feelings of elation when it was announced that the train was approaching Waterloo Station. They had at last reached their intended destination and were looking forward to being greeted by relatives or friends who were awaiting their arrival. Following a 19-day journey that consisted largely of pleasure, the pioneers had been full of hope and optimism, and they were now on the threshold of realising their dream of a better life.

It was however alleged by an individual newcomer of the era that, as the smartly dressed, positivity-filled individuals stepped out of the train and onto the platform at Waterloo Station, they were confronted by a line of men in black shirts:

"Send them back!" the men chanted. "Send them back! Send the niggers back!"

The End

www.ingramcontent.com/pod-product-compliance
Lightning Source LLC
LaVergne TN
LVHW011731060526
838200LV00051B/3135